Eddie Shapes Up

Written by

ED KOCH AND PAT KOCH THALER

Introduction by

PRESIDENT BILL CLINTON

Illustrated by JONATHAN HOEFER

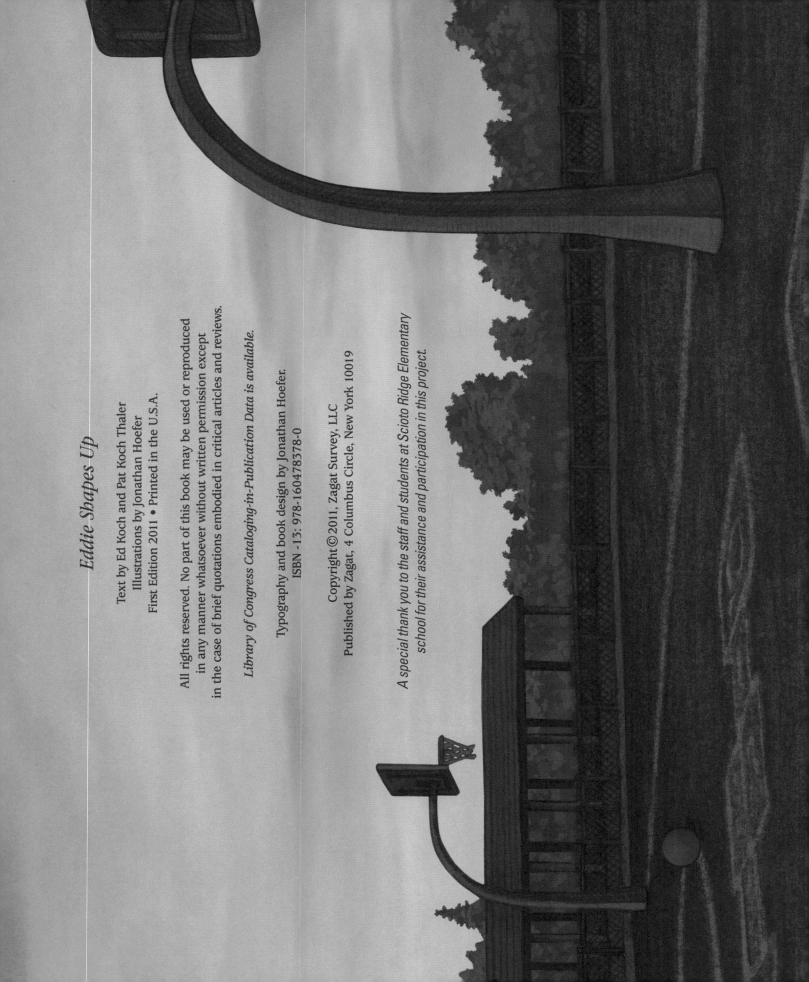

Eddie Shapes Up

Text by Ed Koch and Pat Koch Thaler
Illustrations by Jonathan Hoefer
First Edition 2011 • Printed in the U.S.A.

Library of Congress Cataloging-in-Publication Data is available.

Typography and book design by Jonathan Hoefer.
ISBN -13: 978-160478378-0

Copyright© 2011, Zagat Survey, LLC
Published by Zagat, 4 Columbus Circle, New York 10019

*A special thank you to the staff and students at Scioto Ridge Elementary
school for their assistance and participation in this project.*

by President Bill Clinton

I'm delighted to see books like *Eddie Shapes Up* encouraging children to embrace wellness at an early age. After undergoing two heart surgeries, I knew I would have to change my lifestyle in order to stay well. The rewards of good health have made it all worthwhile. I only wish I had started on this adventure as a young man.

Eddie Shapes Up is a terrific story that shows how, with determination and the encouragement of family and friends, getting healthy can be lots of fun.

For the happy and healthy children in our family.

- E.K. and P.K.T.

Dedicated to my friends and family.

- J.H.

"Eddie, wake up and get ready for school," Mom called.

Eddie turned over and pulled the blanket over his head. Eddie didn't want to go to school this morning. The sun was shining and he was sure there would be recess in the playground.

He peeked out from the covers.

"I can't go to school today. I feel horrible," he called to his mother.

"I have a stomachache, a headache, and my fingers and toes hurt."

Mom came into Eddie's room.

"You don't look sick," she said feeling his forehead. "And you don't have any fever."

"I just don't want to go to school today. We'll have recess outside and I hate recess."

"As far as I know, recess is the part of school that most kids like best. It's a beautiful day. You'll have fun playing outside. Come and have breakfast and then off to school you go."

"You don't understand, Mom,"
Eddie said, pushing the covers
away.

As he was getting dressed, Eddie
noticed that his pants were getting
a little tight.

"They must have shrunk when
they were washed," he thought.

"I'm not too hungry this morning, Mom," Eddie said, coming into the kitchen.

"I'll just have a bagel with butter and eat it on the way. I hope you packed me a big lunch with lots of cookies."

"I think you should have a glass of milk. It's good for you. And cereal or a fruit would be better than a bagel," his mother said.

"No time." Eddie grabbed his books and lunch box and headed out to school.

In class he did well on the spelling test he had studied for the night before.

When the noon buzzer sounded, Eddie sat in the lunchroom with his friends Ben and Noah.

Mom had packed a turkey sandwich, carrot sticks, an apple, and three chocolate cookies. Eddie bought a chocolate milk, threw away the carrots and apple, and gobbled down the sandwich and cookies. He noticed that Ben had some potato chips left over.

"If you're not eating those, I will."

"Let's go outside," Noah said after lunch, sipping from his water bottle. Eddie hung back but there was no point in staying behind. They would close the lunchroom and all the kids would have to go out to the playground.

Ben and Noah joined a game of tag.

"I don't want to run around and get all sweaty," Eddie said when his friends asked him to play. Instead he took his book and sat in a quiet spot against the wall. He tried to read, but was really watching the other kids.

It looked like fun.

Some of the kids playing dodge
ball called over to Eddie.

"Come on and play, fatso," one
boy shouted.

Another shouted, "Come on, slowpoke."

He hated hearing those names and
really didn't want to play because
he always got stuck in the middle.

But they kept calling him.

Eddie reluctantly joined the game. The kid in the middle of the circle threw the ball hard. Eddie tried to get out of the way but was too slow.

BANG.

The ball hit his leg.

Now it was his turn in the middle. The kids danced around and it took five tries for Eddie to finally hit someone.

"I'm not feeling well," he said.

It was just an excuse so he could leave the game.

Noah was watching. With tears in his eyes, Eddie said, "They always try to hit me and I can't get out of the way. And some of the kids call me names. I just won't play anymore."

"You're kind of slow on your feet," Noah said. "That's why they can always hit you with the ball."

"My problem is I never was a fast runner. But that's me. If I were skinny like you instead of, well, chubby, I bet I'd be a great athlete and better at the games."

"Everybody has a different kind of body," Noah replied. "What's important is being healthy and in good shape. And you're definitely not in good shape."

Ben joined them and said, "Look, Eddie. You're our good friend. We like you and we don't want to say anything that will be hurtful. But you are a little heavy and out of shape. Maybe it's because of the way you eat."

"I love food," Eddie replied. "And I know I'll never be thin, so I might as well just eat what I like and as much as I like."

Eddie was hurt by his friends' words, but he knew they were right. He didn't want Ben and Noah to see how upset he was. "I have lots of homework, so I'm going right home after school today. See ya."

Ben called after him.

"Noah and I are going for a run in the park tomorrow. It's Saturday so we have all day and we're trying to get into shape for the soccer season. All three of us are going to play on the after-school team, aren't we? Why don't you meet us in the park?"

"Maybe I'll come," Eddie said.

He didn't think he would and he didn't plan to play soccer.

The next morning, Eddie woke up early.

He had a wonderful dream.

In the dream, he was playing dodge ball. He was light on his feet, quick with the ball, and a star player.

No one could hit him with the ball because he was so fast.

"Eddie," Mom called. "What would you like for breakfast?"

"I'll have milk and cereal and maybe an orange."

Mom smiled to herself. She had been trying to get Eddie to eat healthier foods. This was a good start.

"Mom, I've made up my mind," Eddie said, as he came into the kitchen. "In health class we've been learning about good nutrition, so I have an idea of what I should be eating and how much, and I'm starting right now."

"That's wonderful, Eddie," Mom said as she brought some milk to the table.

After breakfast Eddie met his friends in the park.

"Let's run a little," Ben said, sprinting off down the path. Noah and Eddie followed but Eddie, out of breath, soon stopped.

"Don't worry, Eddie. We've been doing it for a while and it takes time to build up your strength. We'll take it slow."

They walked awhile and then ran for a while.

"Hey, I feel like I'm getting into this," Eddie said breathing hard.

After a while they sat on a bench. Eddie told his friends about his plan to eat healthy and exercise more.

"It's hard to think that I can never eat potato chips or my favorite, chocolate chip cookies, anymore. I can give up a lot of things, but giving up chocolate chip cookies will be really hard."

"You don't have to give up everything – you just have to make sure that most of your diet is healthy," Ben reassured him. "I love pizza, but I only eat one piece – not two or three the way some kids do. Cookies can be a sometimes food."

Getting ready for school the next morning, Eddie asked Mom to put only one cookie into his lunch box with his sandwich and carrot sticks.

"And don't forget my apple, please."

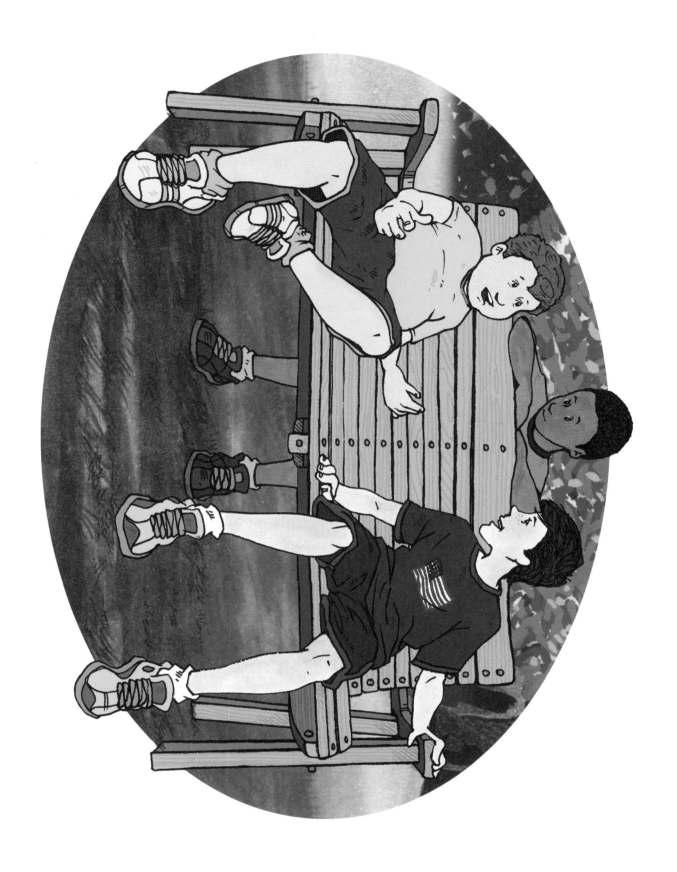

For the next few weeks, Eddie met Ben and Noah in the park after school and on weekends. They walked and ran.

Sometimes they skipped rope and Eddie got really good at that — even better than Ben and Noah.

And soon Eddie was able to keep up when they ran without having to stop for his breath.

One weekend in the park while the boys were resting on a bench, they heard screaming: "My baby! My baby! Help!"

Looking behind them, they saw a baby carriage rolling down the path toward the lake at the bottom of the hill.

Eddie jumped up and ran faster than he ever had before. He grabbed the carriage just before it fell into the lake, baby and all.

The baby's mother came running, tears streaming down her face. She picked the baby up out of the carriage and hugged her.

"Thank you, thank you," she said as she embraced Eddie and kissed him on the cheek. "I fell and the carriage rolled away from me down the path. You saved my baby. You're a hero!"

The next day, Ben and Noah told everyone in school about Eddie's good deed. The boys and girls asked Eddie to tell them how he had saved the baby.

Proudly he told them the whole story.

At recess, Ben and Noah joined the dodge ball game while Eddie stood watching. One of the players pointed to Eddie and called, "You may be a hero, but you're still a slowpoke. Come on. We need someone to hit with the ball."

Eddie took a deep breath and joined the circle. The boy in the middle spotted him and took aim. Everyone moved away from Eddie.

He was the target.

Whiz came the ball, but Eddie moved as fast as he could and the ball missed him. There were several more misses and then – BANG!!!

A particularly good shot hit his arm. He grabbed the ball and went into the middle of the circle. All the kids were running around waving their arms and yelling to Eddie to try and hit them.

Eddie surprised them. He took aim and sent the ball whizzing toward one of the boys who always called him nasty names. It hit the boy and everyone was amazed.

Eddie stayed in the game until recess was over.

As they were going inside Noah said,
"You were fantastic in the game!"

"It was great," Eddie said. "I missed
some but I hit some when I was 'it.'
And guess what? I was able to get out
of the way of the ball lots of times.
It was really fun."

After that, Eddie joined the games
during recess every day. The kids who
had called him names soon grew tired
of doing it when they noticed that it
didn't bother Eddie anymore.

Noah and Ben went to the park every Saturday with Eddie to run and jump rope. They noticed changes in what Eddie ate. Like them, he now ate veggies and fruits for snacks. He still ate cookies, but not as many as before. And he stopped drinking soda and chocolate milk.

When Eddie looked in the mirror in his room at home, he noticed some changes. He certainly wasn't skinny, but his body looked and felt stronger. His clothes weren't tight now. He liked the way he looked.

Now he looked forward to recess – playing dodge ball or tag or jumping rope with the other kids on the playground.

Best of all he played soccer on the team with Noah and Ben.

And he had fun doing it.

A Message to Our Readers

from Ed Koch

As a parent, teacher, or other caregiver, you know that childhood obesity is a growing problem in this country. Perhaps you see signs of it in your own family or observe it in children around you.

I, myself, experienced pain and embarrassment as a chubby child. Frankly, I was more than just a little overweight. Having that body affected me emotionally, socially, and physically. I resisted participating in many games and sports as I was growing up because I was unable to keep up with the other kids. And I was self-conscious about taking off my shirt or putting on a bathing suit in the warm weather.

I loved food and disliked exercise. As a student, I excelled academically and was a great reader. But I was a washout when it came to sports activities and the running and jumping games in the school yard. It was not until I reached high school that I was determined to lose those extra pounds. It was hard work but I succeeded. My regret is that during my pre-teen years, I didn't have the information or motivation to eat in a healthier way and exercise more.

I wish you the children of America a successful and fulfilling life. Success includes the respect of others and enjoying the benefits resulting from that success. Fulfillment means you are doing what makes you feel as though you are achieving your potential and goals in life.

Along the way you should know that your health and physical fitness will play an important role. Our choices and habits control much of what we do in life, so your early choices and habits with respect to eating and exercising should be healthy ones. They will make success and fulfillment more achievable.

All the best.